TURNED ON:

a look at Electricity

by A. Harris Stone
and Bertram M. Siegel

ILLUSTRATED BY PETER P. PLASENCIA

PRENTICE-HALL INC., ENGLEWOOD CLIFFS, N.J.

For
Sid and Mary

Turned On: A Look at Electricity
by A. Harris Stone and Bertram M. Siegel
© 1970 by A. Harris Stone and Bertram M. Siegel

Library of Congress Catalog Card Number: 70-115787
Printed in the United States of America • J
ISBN-0-13-933093-3

Prentice-Hall International, Inc., London
Prentice-Hall of Australia, Pty. Ltd., Sydney
Prentice-Hall of Canada, Ltd., Toronto
Prentice-Hall of India Private Ltd., New Delhi
Prentice-Hall of Japan, Inc., Tokyo

CONTENTS

INTRODUCTION

Sir Isaac Newton was a most accomplished and imaginative scientist. His ideas provided "food for thought" for hundreds of years after his death. He formulated the law of gravity. He described the laws of motion. He set forth the laws of mechanics. Why then did he not, for instance, discover scientific principles related to *current* electricity? Was it because he was not interested? Was it because he did not have the time? Was it because he wasn't smart enough? Was it because nothing was known about electricity during his lifetime?

The answer to these questions is an emphatic No! There was information available to Newton about static electricity which would most likely have stimulated an interest in current electricity. Yet to the best of our knowledge, Newton did not do any work with current electricity. Why? Perhaps it is because of the way knowledge is often obtained.

When a person looks at a body of knowledge, he can *imagine* more than what he can see. Certainly he can see the specific information contained in the statements at which he is looking. For example, in the statement "watt is a quantity of electrical power," he can see bits of specific information—"watt," "quantity," "power." What he doesn't see, and what he must imagine, concerns the time, the place, and the men who took part in developing these specific bits of information.

Who were they? When did they work? How did they make their discoveries? On whose ideas and work did they base their own ideas and work? What difficulties did they have in answering the questions that led them to their discoveries? Were they always the smartest men of their day, or were they sometimes just the luckiest?

In some cases we know a great deal about these men, in other cases very little. But in any case we must know what ideas came before and what ideas came after these men and their work.

Sir Isaac Newton, we can imagine, did not work on current electricity because of the lack of ideas that came before him. Sir Isaac, though brilliant, may have had the handicap of not knowing where to start, also of being unaware that there were questions to ask. Scientists of today, including those beginning scientists who are reading this book, have both the handicaps and the ad-

6

vantages that Newton had. The handicap of not knowing what questions to ask about ideas that have not yet been discovered is the same to all men. One advantage common to all who are willing to read, think, and work is knowing the information that came before them.

This book presents some of the advantages and handicaps that scientists run into every day. You will find some specific information but you will also have to find some questions. You will be able to tell approximately when the questions were first asked and who answered some of them. What you won't find in this book are the questions that will have to come from your own head—and the answers that will have to come from your own work. This book itself is an advantage—it contains ideas for experiments from which you may be able to learn some of the basic principles of electricity. All you have to do is read, work, think—and get *turned on*.

William Gilbert

Magnetism and electricity are closely related. Just playing around with the pieces of equipment shown below will help a beginning experimenter develop an understanding of magnetism.

What phenomena and variations can be observed when the poles of two bar magnets are brought near each other, as shown in the examples below?

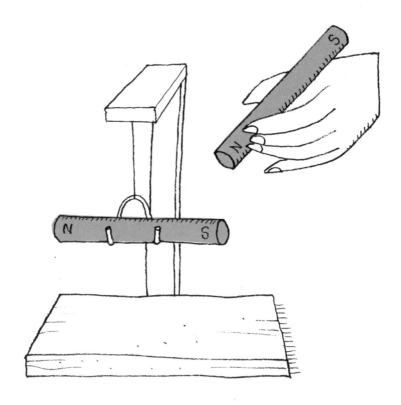

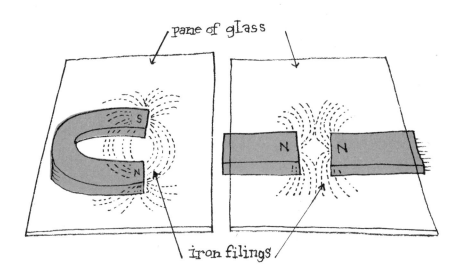

pane of glass

iron filings

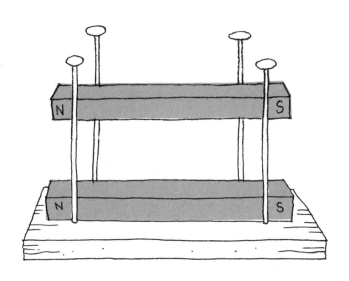

What happens to the magnetic effect when a piece of cardboard is placed between a magnet and a paper clip? Are the results different when paper, aluminum foil, plywood, or a piece of iron are used in place of the cardboard?

Is the magnetic effect changed when the paper clip is placed in a glass of water and the magnet is held outside the glass?

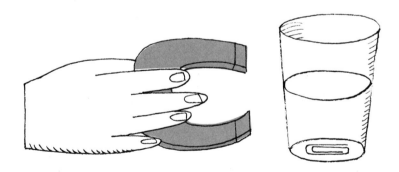

The change in magnetic effect that is seen when various materials are placed between a magnet and a magnetic object can be measured. The apparatus shown below can be used with several sheets of paper between the fixed bottom plate and the movable magnet. How many sheets should be used between the magnet and the plate to make the scale show the greatest amount of force needed to separate the magnet from the plate?

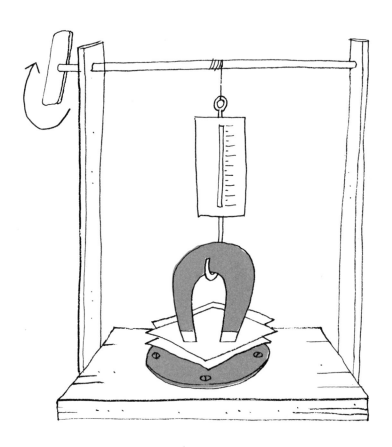

What is the relationship between the number of sheets of paper used and the force needed to separate the magnet from the plate? This question can be answered by plotting the "force of separation" on one axis of a graph and the number of sheets of paper used on the other axis.

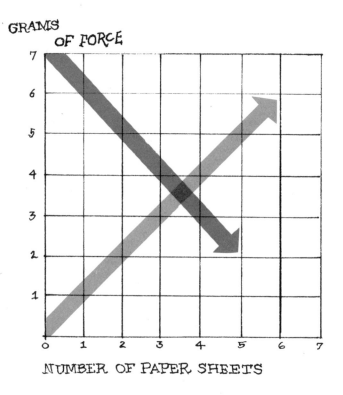

How can you determine whether it is the material between the magnet and the object or the distance between the magnet and the object that is responsible for the observed effect?

The relationship between a bar magnet and a compass may be determined when a magnet is suspended as shown below. Toward what direction does the north pole of the magnet point?

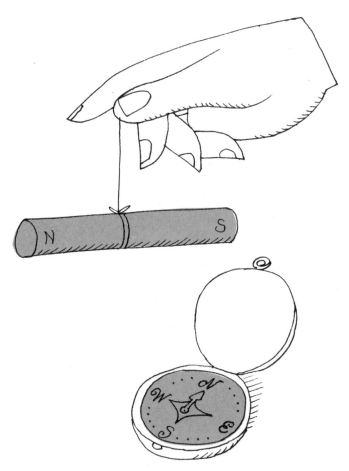

If the south pole of a magnet points south, does this mean that similar poles attract?

The effect observed when the magnet of a compass, often called the needle, points north is only one of the effects of the earth on magnets. The apparatus pictured below will be helpful in learning about the relationship between a magnet and your location on the earth.

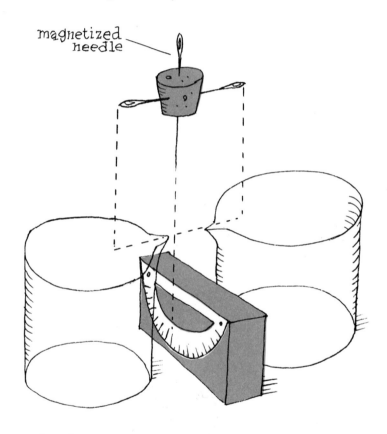

magnetized needle

Why should the apparatus be set up so that the magnetized needle is lined up in a north-south line? What is the dip angle (the angle that an inclined magnet makes with the horizontal) at your latitude? What would be the dip angle at the north pole, At the equator?

Though they were not the first to know of magnets and magnetism, the Greeks told of metal spears and arrows being attracted and sticking to certain minerals that came to be called lodestone. Lodestone is known today as the mineral *magnetite*. Compasses were first made from lodestone and were used by sailors as a navigational aid. Later it was discovered that metal rubbed with lodestone had the same effect. But how and why compasses worked as they did was not known.

Most early scientists thought that magnetic compasses were controlled and directed by the North Star. Today this explanation is considered unsuitable. But what makes one explanation better than another? Does the idea of the North Star controlling magnets explain what was observed? And if an explanation works, why is it rejected only to be replaced by another explanation? Perhaps those who thought that magnets were controlled by the North Star were in the same position as Newton was with current electricity. Could it be that neither knew what questions to ask?

In 1600 Sir William Gilbert, an English scientist, proposed another explanation for the effects of magnetic compasses. He assumed that if the earth was a magnet with a north and south pole, it would attract the poles of a magnet. While this explanation is not fully accepted today, we talk in terms of the earth's north pole and south pole. The ideas of Gilbert led to today's understanding of magnetic phenomena.

Otto Von Guericke

Static electricity is one kind of electrical energy that was studied by early scientists. What happens when large amounts of static electricity are produced? A static generator for making large quantities of static charges is shown here. This device, often called an *electrophorous,* can be made by filling a metal pie plate with melted sealing wax and attaching an aluminum disc to a piece of broomstick. Charge the electrophorous by rubbing the cooled wax with a piece of fur or silk.

CAUTION: HAVE AN ADULT HELP YOU MELT THE WAX!

a.

b.

c.

What happens when you put your finger near the metal disc?

Electricity and magnets are closely related. What happens as a rod charged with static electricity is moved close to a similarly charged rod that is part of a *balanced* soda straw balance? The charged rod can be made by rubbing a glass rod with a silk scarf. How far away from the balanced rod is the hand-held rod when it first begins to produce an effect?

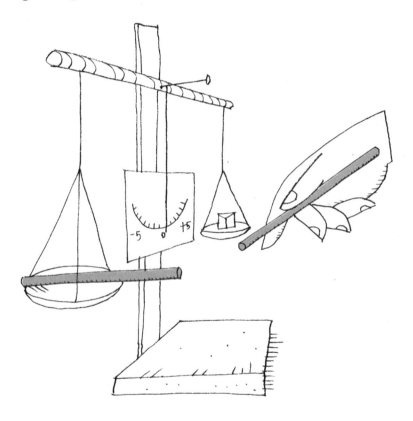

Does rubbing the rod for a longer time produce a "larger" effect? Is the distance at which the rods begin to move greater when there is a larger charge?

How can you know that you have produced large quantities of static electricity? The apparatus shown below is called an electroscope and is useful in answering this question.

What relationship can be found between the amount of time you spent rubbing the wax plate, and the distance the "leaves" move when the aluminum disc of the electrophorous is brought near the jar?

Can an electroscope be made with paper leaves? Rubber leaves?

What is it that enables one student to get A's in every subject, to play on the school's football, baseball and basketball teams, to be president of the student council, to be a scout, and to study a musical instrument? How can one girl be on the honor roll, have the lead in the school play, be a cheerleader, and still have time to be a volunteer worker in a hospital? What makes one person able to have so many different interests and excel in each interest? Is it genius? Is it hard work? Thomas Edison claimed that "Genius is ninety-nine percent perspiration and one percent inspiration."

Otto von Guericke is a good example of a man with a variety of interests. He designed one of the first machines to produce static electricity. He became famous for his experiments with air and air pressure. At the same time, he was mayor of the German city of Magdeburg in which he worked. Von Guericke lived and worked in the 1600s. Is study, experimenting, and working in many different areas still possible today?

Pieter Musschenbroek

Static electricity, which is closely related to magnetism, can be produced, detected, and *stored*. The *Leyden jar* is used for the storage of static charge. Can you use an electroscope to find out how much static charge is still in the jar after one hour? Try to detect the remaining stored static charge after four hours, eight hours, and twenty-four hours.

A Leyden jar may be made by coating the inside and outside of a jar with aluminum paint. *A bare wire is used to transport the static charge to the coated suface; the Leyden jar should be placed on a second bare wire.*

CAUTION: TOUCHING A LEYDEN JAR MAY PRODUCE A SHOCK!

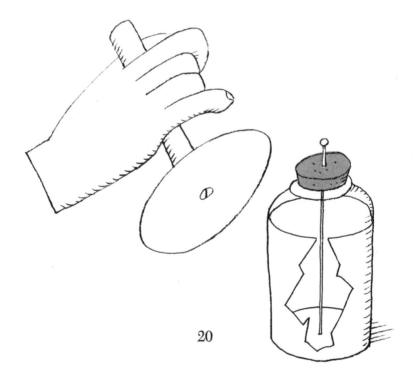

By 1746 much was known about electricity, how it behaved, and how it interacted with different materials. However, despite this knowledge, friction machines were being used only to make bigger sparks. A new discovery was needed. A device was required that could store up electrical charges.

The story is told that while attempting to use a friction machine to put a charge on a container of water he held in his hand, Professor Musschenbroek touched the conductor between the container and machine with his other hand, with very shocking results. The Professor began experimenting with his device which soon became known as the Leyden jar, named after the university in Holland where he worked.

Today's relative of the Leyden jar is called a *condenser* or a *capacitor*. Radio and television tubes and many electrical and electronic circuits could not function without these devices to store and discharge electricity.

Hans Oersted

The relationship between electric current and magnetism can be studied by using the apparatus shown below. What happens when the metal core wrapped in a coil of wire attached to a battery is moved along a meter stick toward a compass?

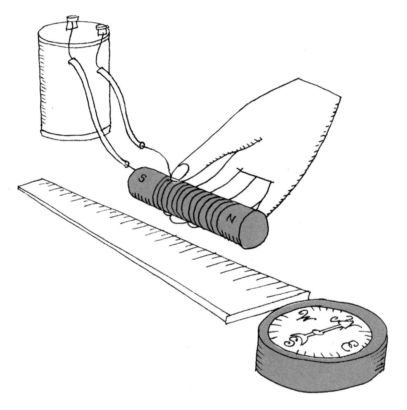

Does the number of turns of wire around the metal core affect what is seen? What effect does using more than one battery have on what is seen?

Try using cores of iron, brass, steel, carbon, and wood.

Type of core	# of turns of wire	# of batteries	Distance of magnet from compass when needle first moves
iron	10	1	?
		2	?
	20	1	?
		2	?
		1	?
brass	10	2	?
		1	?
	20	2	?
		1	?
steel	10	2	?
		1	?
	20	2	?
		1	?
carbon	10	2	?
		1	?
	20	2	?
		1	?
wood	10	2	?
		1	?
	20	2	?
		1	?
air	10	2	?
		1	?
	20	2	?
		1	?
aluminum	10	2	?
		1	?
	20	2	?

Cores of different materials produce different effects on what can be seen. What ideas can be used to explain the effect of an "air" core? What material should be used as a core in order to build the most powerful electromagnet?

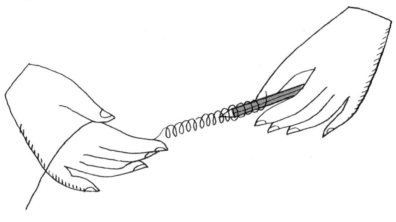

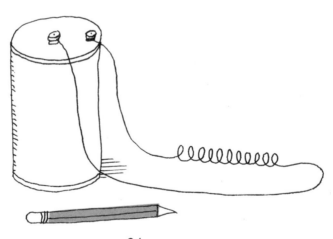

A compass, a wire coiled around a pencil, a yardstick, and a battery can be used to find out how distance alone affects the interaction of an object and a magnetic field. Try holding the compass 30 inches, 25 inches, 20 inches, 15 inches, 10 inches, and 5 inches from the pencil coil.

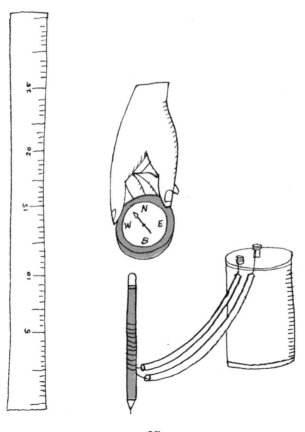

Does the strength of the magnetic field change or does the relationship between the pencil coil and compass change?

A compass, a length of wire, a battery, and curiosity were the tools that led Hans Oersted to discover that an electric current is accompanied by a magnetic field. The Danish scientist, who is honored by having the unit of magnetic intensity named for him, made this discovery in 1819.

Oersted's discovery, much like that of Musschenbroek's occurred almost by accident. The history of science is full of stories of "accidental" discoveries. But were they really accidental? Is there some set of conditions in a man's mind that makes it more likely for him to stumble onto a discovery than someone else? Could some other scientist have made the same discovery as Oersted? Let's guess what the conditions might have been that led Oersted to be the first to find the relationship between electricity and magnetism.

Did Oersted have a lot of miscellaneous information that suddenly came together in a blinding flash of insight?

Was he working on some other problem when he accidentally discovered this relationship?

Is it possible that he got upset with his family and was working in anger that day he first saw the relationship? And that this anger had an effect on his thinking?

Could it be that Oersted was a very methodic man who eliminated all other solutions to the problem?

What is the chance that Oersted had a laboratory assistant who gave him the idea he later developed?

It is impossible now to know exactly what happened in Oersted's mind that led him to make his discovery, but it is interesting to think about how a man operates when he is *turned on!*

Alessandro Volta

Static electricity is not the kind of electricity that lights lamps and runs household appliances. Jobs like this are done by the kind of electricity that is called *current electricity*. How can the presence of current electricity be detected? What happens when a dry cell is connected to an insulated wire coiled around a compass?

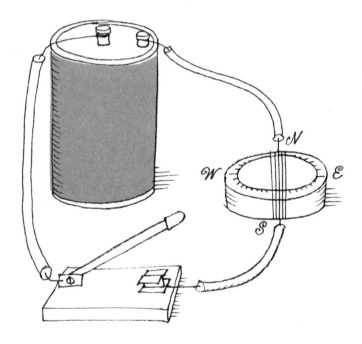

How does connecting several dry cells affect what is seen? Does increasing the number of turns of wire around the compass have any effect on the number of *arbitrary units* measured?

The dry cell is only one way of producing current electricity. Other kinds of cells can be made by using various metals together with acid, base, or salt solutions. Which cell produces the greatest effect on the wire-coiled-compass indicator? One made by copper and zinc strips in vinegar or the dry cell?

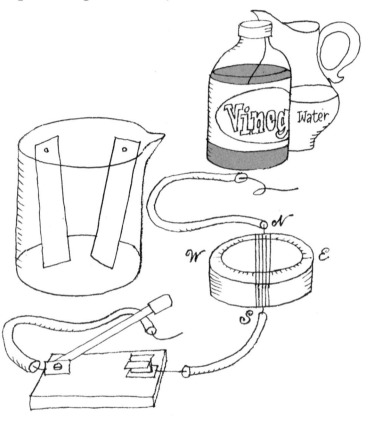

Does a cell made by using copper and carbon in vinegar produce as much current as one made of zinc and carbon?

"Wet" cells can be made by using different combinations of *electrodes*. Which combination of electrodes *in vinegar* produces the greatest effect on the wired-compass indicator? The least effect?

electrodes	effect in arbitrary units
copper with_____	?
zinc with_____	?
carbon with_____	?
aluminum with_____	?
steel with_____	?
silver with_____	?

What effect does using two strips of each metal have on the amount of current produced? Does the quantity of vinegar that is used have any effect on the amount of current produced?

Electrodes are only one important part of a wet cell. The liquid used in the cell is also an important factor. The acid, base, or salt solutions used in wet cells are called *electrolytes*. Which of the following electrolytes produces the greatest effect on the wired compass when used with copper and zinc electrodes?

30

electrolyte	effect in arbitrary units
salt in water	?
baking soda in water	?
sugar in water	?
liquid soap in water	?
detergent in water	?
cola soda	?
water	?
lemon juice	?

Humphry Davy

What happens to the water in two test tubes when an electrode attached to a battery is placed in each tube? How does adding salt to the water affect what happens? Adding lemon juice?

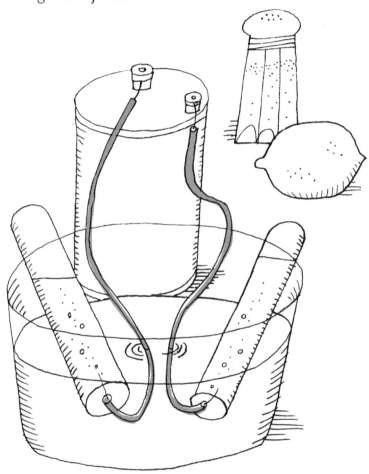

Does using more than one battery affect what happens?

A *possible* explanation of what happens to the water in the test tube is that the electric current pushed the water back into the container. Before designing an experiment, using the same apparatus, to disprove this explanation, you might ask some questions. What *did* happen to the water in the tubes? Was the same amount of water affected in both tubes? Is it possible to prove that something is in the tubes?

Volta's "piles" became experimental tools for many scientists. Humphry Davy, an English scientist, was one of the many who based his work on that of Volta and Galvani. In 1800 Davy experimented with the electrolysis of water. He found that the amounts of gases produced by running an electric current through water occurred in approximately a two-to-one ratio. That is, there was always twice as much of one gas as there was of another. By testing and identifying these gases, Davy was able to describe the composition of water.

But what happened to the water in the tubes?

Michael Faraday

A study of how scientists *measure* and *estimate* can be made by using the apparatus shown on the opposite page. When building this apparatus, do not be afraid to use substitutes for any of the equipment that you have trouble finding.

It is often difficult for scientists to make accurate measurements of phenomena. Yet, these measurements are almost always needed to understand what has happened. Even though measurements may be difficult to make at first, scientists always try to find a way to collect numbers that represent how fast, how much, or how many. Until they decide on an exact way to measure what happens, they have to estimate. Before the speed of an electric motor is measured, for instance, it can be estimated.

Estimate the speed of the centerpiece of the motor when one battery is used; when two batteries are used; when thirty turns of wire are used on each end; when sixty turns are used.

ESTIMATED SPEED IN REVOLUTIONS
PER MINUTE

Trial #	One battery	Two batteries	30 turns	60 turns
1				
2				
3				
4				

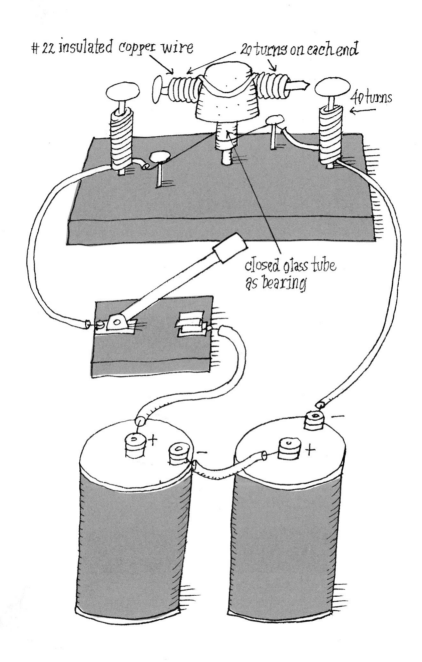

22 insulated copper wire

20 turns on each end

40 turns

closed glass tube
as bearing

Estimating is important. But measuring accurately is a constant goal. Several devices can be built to measure the speed of an electric motor. One such apparatus is shown below.

The factors most critical in designing the apparatus so that it works are:

1. how fast the roll of paper is pulled;
2. the amount of weight on the recording arm;
3. the type of writing instrument on the recording arm;
4. the kind of support used for the recording arm.

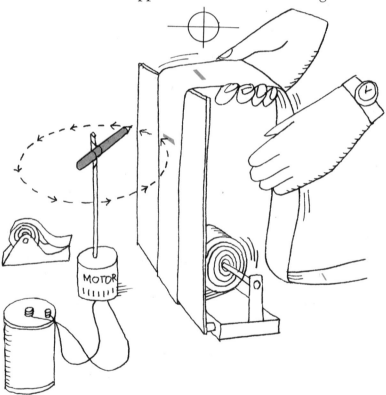

Oersted discovered a relationship between electricity and magnetism. Ampère, Davy, and others experimented with Oersted's idea. But it was not until Faraday discovered a second relationship that men could actually begin to use electricity.

Faraday's ideas of electrical *induction* led the way to the development of the enormous generators found in today's electrical plants. His dynamo was the first electrical generator. The dynamo made it possible to "manufacture" a steady, controlled flow of electricity. Static machines, Leyden jars, and other devices were fine as experimental tools, but with the invention of Faraday's generator, discovery and invention of electrical instruments came at a very rapid rate. Improved Faraday coils were used by Hertz to generate the first wireless waves. This discovery led to the development of radio. The telegraph, street lights, and the phonograph soon followed.

IN THE AIR

Does the design of a circuit have any effect on the amount of current that flows through it? A wired-compass indicator will be helpful in determining the amount of current flowing through the circuits shown below. Try using three flashlight bulbs as resistors.

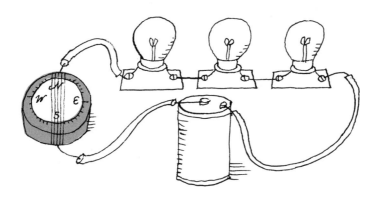

Does the location of the resistors in the test circuit have any effect on the amount of current detected? Now try this circuit:

Circuit	Location	Amount of current in arbitrary units
1	A	
	B	
	C	
	D	
2	A	
	B	
	C	
	D	

How does the number of bulb resistors used in each circuit affect the amount of current that flows through the circuit?

The relationship between a circuit and a fuse can be determined by using single strands of picture-hanging wire and the apparatus shown below.

CAUTION: ASK AN ADULT TO ASSIST YOU IN BLOWING YOUR FUSES.

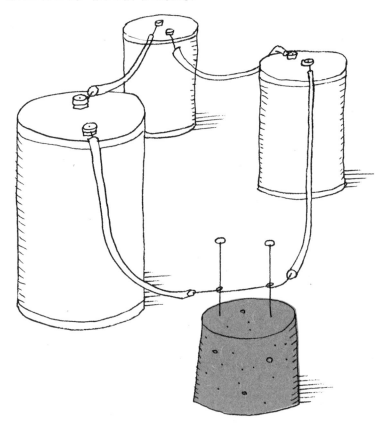

What is the effect on the circuit if four strands of wire are used as a fuse? Eight? Sixteen? Thirty-two strands? Does the number of batteries used have an effect on the number of strands of "fuse" needed?

The identity of the discoverers of the wheel and the lever have been lost in the history of man. Whatever flash of insight the discoverer may have had or how many hours and days he labored in developing his idea has been lost along with his name. But there can be no question of how much we owe these unknown discoverers.

Who was the first man to design a series circuit? A parallel circuit? Who was the first person to use a device to prevent a circuit from becoming too hot? The answers to these questions seem to be lost, as have the names of the discoverers of the wheel and lever. The answer to another question—"what led these discoverers to design circuits?"—has also been lost. What ideas were these men working on when they connected wires and resistors in such designs? Were they concerned about circuits or were these circuits needed to determine something else? Did these discoverers set out to discover circuits and fuses or was the idea "in the air"?

André Ampère

The apparatus below is made by using a "wired-compass meter," a battery, and some wire in a salt water solution. How does the current flow from A to B?

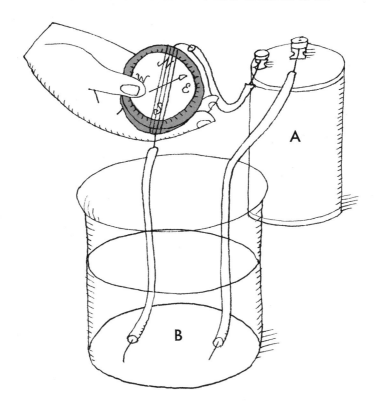

What happens between A and B? Develop models and ideas to explain what happens. Try these:
1. A little man is invisibly holding the wires together.
2. Glass conducts electricity.
3. Current exists.
4.   ?

Advanced mathematics, mechanics, electricity, magnetism, theory of gases, particle physics, animal physiology, theory of the earth, psychology, and philosophy are some of the areas that André Ampère studied, experimented in, and wrote about. Best known for his work in electricity, this French scientist made discoveries which developed into devices such as the electric bell, all electric motors and generators, radio and television.

Often called the Newton of electricity, Ampère first noted the relationships between an electric current and magnetism. From this, he then discovered the magnetic relationships in straight and coiled wires.

Perhaps one of his most imaginative articles deals with a theory of magnetism. This theory explains magnetism by assuming that each particle within the magnetic substance acted like a magnet. This idea of "molecular electricity" was published in 1823.

Georg Ohm

What is the effect on the amount of current flowing through a circuit when the resistance is increased? How can this effect be seen or measured? These questions can be studied by first seeing what happens to a light bulb when an electric train transformer is used as a power source to light the bulb.

CAUTION: BE SURE AN ADULT IS AROUND TO HELP YOU.

What are the resistances in a bulb-wire transformer circuit? How is it possible to judge the brightness of the bulb?

If you have learned to judge bulb brightness and to relate it to the amount of resistance in a transformer-wire-bulb circuit, then you can judge which of several *insulated* wires is the "best" to use in circuits. Which of the following offers the most resistance? The least? Iron? Copper? Nichrome? Aluminum?

ASK THAT NICE ADULT TO HELP YOU AGAIN.

The apparatus shown below may be helpful in answering these questions.

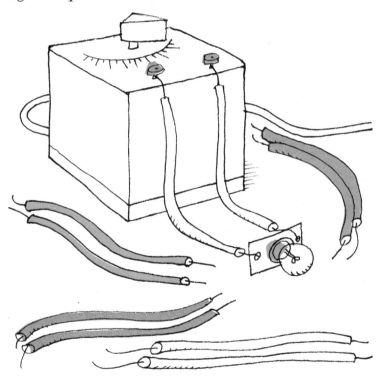

How does the thickness of the wire affect the brightness of the bulb?

How accurate were the estimates you made on bulb brightness? Using a battery, wires of different resistance, and a wired-compass meter, you can place the wires in order of increasing resistance. Try *insulated* wires of aluminum, Nichrome, copper, and steel.

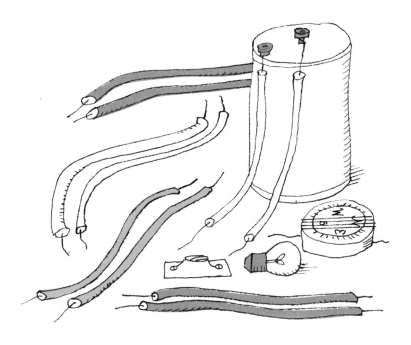

	Resistance	Meter Reading
Highest	1	?
	2	?
	3	?
	4	?
Lowest	5	?

What is the possibility of measuring something that cannot be seen? Instruments can be built that show the presence of invisible forces. These forces are known to exist only because of the way they affect other forces or materials. But the ability to detect a force is very different from measuring that force. Answers to questions such as "how strong?" "how much?" or "how many?" require units or systems of measurements. And measurements are needed to build relationships. Measurements of electricity are no exception.

The components or parts of an electrical system include the intensity of the electrical current (amperes), the amount of electrical current (volts), and the resistance offered by the wires or parts of the circuit. Georg Ohm first conceived of the idea that each current has a definite pressure or intensity and that the circuit itself offers resistance to the amount of current that flows through it. Because of his work, we now measure resistance in units called *ohms*.

What is the relationship between the *intensity* of an electrical current, the *amount* of current, and the *resistance* offered?

To study a system, you must often study its component parts. An electrical connection is no exception. What are the relationships between the parts of this system? If one of the factors that make up the system changes, will the entire system change?

Joseph Henry

One way that the knowledge about electricity and magnetism has been put to use by man is in the telegraph. What is the relationship between magnetism and electricity in the apparatus shown below?

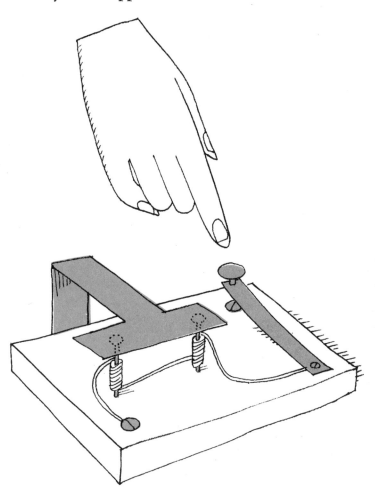

Who "owns" a discovery? Does the discoverer have all the rights to it? What about the man who used that discovery to make a different device? Does the man who demonstrates a device and suggests that it could be used to make a second device have any right to the second device? Should the man who uses another man's ideas give a share of his credit and wealth to the first man?

In 1821 Joseph Henry published an article describing how he had perfected an electromagnet and battery capable of magnetizing iron at a great distance. Henry also pointed out that it was now possible to invent an electromagnet telegraph. But he did not bother to patent his magnets.

By 1884, Henry's magnetic system was improved, adapted, and altered. The combined efforts of Samuel Morse, his two assistants, and, on occasion, Henry himself resulted in a reliable working telegraph system. The question is, who invented the telegraph?

The questions "How much light is there?" and "How bright is it?" can be answered with a photoelectric photometer—often called a photographer's light meter. A lamp, yardstick, and light meter will help you find out what effect distance has on the *intensity* of light. Before starting, ask someone to show you how to use a light meter.

CAUTION: BOTH LIGHT METERS AND THE ADULT OWNERS FROM WHOM THEY ARE BORROWED MUST BE HANDLED GENTLY!

Watts of bulb	Distance in meter or feet	Meter reading
	4	?
	8	?
50	16	?
	32	?
	4	?
	8	?
75	16	?
	32	?
	4	?
	8	?
100	16	?
	32	?

Does the color of light have any effect on its intensity? Try the experiment on the opposite page with different colored pieces of cellophane in front of the bulb. Does doubling the wattage of the bulb have the same effect here as it did in the experiment on the opposite page?

CAUTION: DO NOT LET THE CELLOPHANE TOUCH THE BULB; IT IS HIGHLY FLAMMABLE.

Watts of bulb	Color of cellophane	Distance in meters or feet	Meter reading
50	Red	4	?
		8	?
		16	?
		32	?
	Yellow	4	?
		8	?
		16	?
		32	?
	Green	4	?
		8	?
		16	?
		32	?
75	Red	4	?
		8	?
		16	?
		32	?
	Yellow	4	?
		8	?
		16	?
		32	?
	Green	4	?
		8	?
		16	?
		32	?

What is "enough light"? Is the amount of light you need when you build a model enough light to read by? Is the amount of light you use when you eat, enough light to read by? What effect do people say they get from "too much" light or "bright" light? How much light is too much to eat by? To read by? To watch television by?

The answer to the question, "What causes the needle of a light meter to move when light shines on it?" is a perfect example of how scientists share and build upon each other's ideas.

Heinrich Hertz was studying spark discharges between two metal spheres. He observed that the discharges occurred more rapidly when the spheres were lit by another spark discharge. This observation was the discovery of the *photoelectric effect*. Max Planck, another German scientist, proposed a theory dealing with the way particles of matter absorb energy. Were these two ideas different? One is an observation and one a theory, with no *apparent* relationship between them. It remained for Albert Einstein, in 1905, to use Planck's theory to explain Hertz's observations. For this important *synthesis* of ideas, Einstein was honored with one of the greatest scientific awards, the Nobel Prize.

Today, photographic or "light" meters and "electric eyes" use the photoelectric effect to open doors, set off alarm systems, and set camera lenses.

Thomas Seebeck

What is the relationship between heat energy and current electricity, as observed by using the apparatus shown below?

CAUTION: HAVE AN ADULT HELP YOU HEAT THE WIRES.

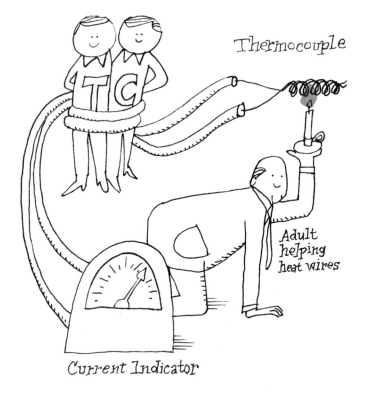

Current Indicator

What effect does using two copper wires instead of one copper wire and one iron wire have on what is seen?

What effect does room temperature have on the current indicator reading? Does using two candles have any effect on what occurs?

The effect observed when heat is applied to the point where two wires of different metals are joined was first discovered in 1822. The Seebeck effect, as this phenomenon is called, is named for its discoverer, the German scientist Thomas J. Seebeck. The devise used to produce the Seebeck effect is often called a *thermocouple*.

The thermocouple has many uses. One use is as a source of electricity. Another involves using the thermocouple as a regulator of electrical current. In many devices thermocouples are used as thermometers. Heat energy is transformed into electrical energy in the Seebeck effect. If scientists know how much heat is required to produce a certain amount of electricity, they can calibrate a thermocouple to act as a thermometer that measures heat in units of electrical current.

ON BEING TURNED ON!

How do men make discoveries? Are there some special ways, some mystical secrets known to only a few? Or are there tried and true pathways to success in scientific discovery? In fact, does anyone know how discoveries are made?

Certainly there must be some general ideas that can be related to the large number of scientific discoveries that have been made in the last hundred years. A look at some of these general ideas may help to develop some understanding of the problems faced by scientists and would-be scientists.

Where do ideas come from and how do they get from where they started to where they end? Ideas are the products of men's minds and no matter how they are passed along, they can only be passed from one man to another. When the sciences were very young, there were only a few men who could be called scientists. These men were not next-door neighbors, so passing information from one to another was a difficult task. As an example, in the year 1600, Gilbert formulated ideas about the earth being a magnet. Even though his ideas were a matter of record, it took many years for these ideas to reach other scientists and for them to react to them. It was not until more than two hundred years later that Faraday, perhaps drawing upon Gilbert's ideas, developed his dynamo model of the earth. But Faraday may not have been able to develop his ideas without the work of another scientist who came between him and Gilbert. This scientist was Hans Oersted. Oersted provided what may have been a link between the ideas of Gilbert and those of Faraday. The two hundred years between Gilbert and Faraday was a very long period compared to the rate at which scientific ideas develop today. The reason for this time lag may well be that the development of scientific ideas and discoveries is very much dependent on the transmission of ideas and discoveries from one man to another. It seems clear then that at least one major step in the process of making discoveries is the transmission of ideas.

Is it true that the more ideas there are to draw upon, the more ideas there are to be developed? A look at the number of discoveries made by modern science seems to answer "yes" to this question. But where there are more ideas, it is probably true that there are more men thinking up these ideas. For example, today there are more scientists working more closely together on more different projects and generating more new ideas than ever before. Since there are more scientists working together, it is easier for them to pass information to each other more rapidly. So it seems that a second factor on which discoveries depend is the production of ideas—the more ideas generated, the more new ideas will grow from them.

Scientific equipment and the growth of *technology* also play a role in the development of ideas. As men produce more ideas about the scientific world, there is an increasingly greater need to test the value of these ideas and to determine their correctness. It is only through experimentation that science can sort out which ideas are most valuable and which need to be restudied. Only the strongest and most supportable ideas can withstand the tests of experimentation. So a third factor in the development of scientific ideas seems to be the ability to experiment to verify the strength of each idea.

Science is what scientists do. Since all of the people who engage in these activities depend upon each other for information, it is understandable that they make the same discoveries at the same time. Certainly they all have the same information available, they all use similar kinds of equipment, and they all share the ideas that they are working on while they are working on them. In fact, it would be strange if simultaneous discoveries were not constantly being made.

So far we have looked at many of the factors which are essential to the making of discoveries. But we have not answered the question we first asked, "How do men make discoveries?" Perhaps it is because the making of discoveries is a very individual and personal happening. No one knows which scientist or which would-be scientist will make the next breakthrough discovery. The person who does make this discovery may already be a scientist. Or he may be reading this book.

GLOSSARY

AMPERE   The unit used for measuring electric current is the ampere. One ampere is the amount of electricity in a circuit where the electrical pressure is one volt and the reistance is one ohm.

AMPÈRE, ANDRÉ (1775–1836)   This French physicist first introduced the terms "electrostatics" and "electrodynamics" and also invented the term "galvanometer" for current-measuring devices. Because of his discovery of electric currents and their causes, the unit of electric current, the ampere, was named for him.

BATTERY   Two or more cells connected in either series or parallel form a battery. A flashlight battery is actually one cell.

CAPACITOR   A capacitor is an electrical device made up of two conductors separated by an insulator.

CELL   In physics, a cell is a container in which electrodes in an electrolytic solution generate electricity.

CHARGE   An object is charged when an excess of positive or negative electricity is produced on the object by its being rubbed with another object.

CIRCUIT   A circuit is a complete pathway through which electricity passes.

COMPASS   A compass is an instrument used to determine direction, usually consisting of a magnetic needle supported so that it can turn freely under the influence of the earth's magnetic field.

CONDENSER   A condenser is a device for storing electric charges. See capacitor.

CONDUCTOR   Any substance that transmits energy, such as heat, sound, or electricity, without the substance itself moving.

CURRENT   The flow or movement of electric charges is called an electric current.

DAVY, HUMPHRY (1778–1829)   Davy, an English chemist, decomposed many chemical substances by electrolysis, isolating potassium, sodium, and calcium. In 1821 he hired Michael Faraday as his laboratory assistant.

DIP ANGLE   Dip angle, often called magnetic inclination or magnetic dip, is the angle that an inclined magnet makes with the horizontal. This effect varies from place to place on the earth's surface.

EINSTEIN, ALBERT (1879–1955)   The most outstanding physicist of the twentieth century was born in Germany and came to the United States in 1933. Dr. Einstein was awarded the Nobel Prize in 1921 for his photoelectric laws.

ELECTRODE   The terminal in an electric circuit that connects the conductor with another conducting substance is called an electrode.

ELECTROLYSIS   Electrolysis is the process by which a chemical compound in solution is decomposed by the action of an electric current passing through the solution.

ELECTROLYTE   An electrolyte is a compound that in solution or in a molten state conducts electricity. An electrolyte is also a conducting solution that contains such a compound.

ELECTROMAGNETIC INDUCTION Voltage is produced by electromagnetic induction when a conductor in a closed circuit moves across magnetic lines of force.

ELECTROPHOROUS An electrophorous is a piece of apparatus used in a laboratory to obtain a number of charges of static electricity from a single initial charge.

ELECTROSCOPE An electroscope is an instrument that detects small charges of electricity.

FARADAY, MICHAEL (1791–1867) This self-educated English physicist and chemist published his first scientific report at the age of sixteen and was one of the most productive researchers of all time. Some of his far-reaching discoveries resulted from his work on electromagnetic induction.

FUSE A fuse is a protective device that opens an electric circuit when a dangerously large current flows through it. Fuses protect circuits from overheating and causing fires.

GILBERT, WILLIAM (1544–1603) Gilbert's theory that the earth is a magnet opened up the studies of terrestrial magnetism. This English physicist also first distinguished between electrical and magnetic attraction.

HENRY, JOSEPH (1797–1878) This American physicist, working independently, discovered self-induction and produced and demonstrated an electromagnetic telegraph. Henry became the first director of the Smithsonian Institution.

INDUCTION Induction is the production of an electric charge or a magnetic field in an object when that object is near an electrically charged body or in a magnetic field originating in another object.

61

INSULATOR   An insulator is a material used to prevent or reduce the passage of heat, electricity, or sound from one area or substance to another.

INTENSITY   Intensity is an expression of the concentration of force or energy or in a given area, volume, or period of time. Intensity usually decreases as the distance from the source increases.

LEYDEN JAR   The Leyden jar was an early form of condenser used in many of the original experiments in electrostatics.

MAGNET   A magnet is often defined as any object that will attract iron by a force other than electrical, gravitational, or nuclear.

MAGNETIC FIELD   The space around a magnet or a conductor carrying electric current in which magnetic effects can be seen is a magnetic field.

MAGNETIC INDUCTION   Magnetic induction is the phenomenon by which an electric current is produced in a conductor moving through a magnetic field. It's also the phenomenon by which an unmagnetized object becomes a magnet when placed in a magnetic field.

MAGNETISM   Those events that occur within or are caused by a magnetic field are called magnetism. Scientists have not yet explained the exact causes of magnetism.

MORSE, SAMUEL FINLEY BREESE (1791–1872)   Morse, an American artist and inventor, patented the first workable telegraphic apparatus and invented the system of dots and dashes that became the Morse code.

MUSSCHENBROEK, PIETER (1692–1761) A Dutch physicist, Musschenbroek worked extensively in the fields of electricity and magnetism. His Leyden jar was the first device used for storing electricity.

OERSTED, HANS (1777–1851) The discovery by this Danish physicist that an electric current can deflect a compass needle was developed by Ampère and formed the foundations for the science of electromagnetism.

OHM, GEORG (1787–1854) This German physicist is best known for his formulation of the mathematical relationship between potential difference, current, and resistance.

OHM Named after Georg Ohm, the ohm is the unit used to measure electric resistance.

PHOTOELECTRIC EFFECT The photoelectric effect is the action by which an electric current is generated in certain substances as a result of absorbing light energy.

PHOTOMETER A photometer, also called a light meter, is an instrument used to measure the intensity of light.

RESISTANCE Resistance is the opposition offered by a material to a flow of electricity through the material.

SEEBECK EFFECT The Seebeck effect is observed when the junction of two dissimilar metals is heated and an electric current is produced.

SEEBECK, THOMAS J. (1770–1831) This German physicist discovered the thermocouple and thermoelectricity in 1822.

STATIC ELECTRICITY   Any electric charge that is not in motion is a static charge. Static charges are usually induced on non-conducting material such as rubber or glass.

SYNTHESIS   Synthesis is the putting together or combining of parts or elements to make a whole.

TECHNOLOGY   Sometimes called "applied science," technology is that branch of human activity dealing with application of science to practical purposes.

THERMOELECTRICITY   Thermoelectricity is the production of electricity by the application of heat to the junction of dissimilar metals. This phenomenon is also known as the thermoelectric or Seebeck effect.

VOLT   The volt is a unit of electric force required to cause a steady flow of current of one ampere to flow through a resistance of one ohm.

VOLTA, ALESSANDRO (1745–1827)   In addition to inventing the electrophorous, this Italian physicist developed a theory of metallic electricity which led him to the discovery of the electric cell.

VON GUERICKE, OTTO (1602–1686)   When mayor of Magdeburg, Germany, Von Guericke experimented with air pumps and also invented one of the first electrostatic generators.

WATT   A watt is the power produced when one ampere of current flows between two points with a force of one volt.